DATE

DICTIONARY WORDS

As you read this book, you will find that some words
are darker black ink than others on the page. You should
look up the meaning of these words in your dictionary,
if you do not already know them.

OTHER TITLES IN THE SERIES

Based on William Shakespeare's

Hamlet

Jennifer Bassett
Series Editor Derek Strange

PENGUIN ENGLISH

To Richard,
who lived through it

PENGUIN ENGLISH

Published by the Penguin Group
Penguin Books Ltd, 27 Wrights Lane, London W8 5TZ, England
Penguin Books USA Inc., 375 Hudson Street, New York, New York 10014, USA
Penguin Books Australia Ltd, Ringwood, Victoria, Australia
Penguin Books Canada Ltd, 10 Alcorn Avenue, Toronto, Ontario, Canada M4V 3B2
Penguin Books (NZ) Ltd, 182–190 Wairau Road, Auckland 10, New Zealand

Penguin Books Ltd, Registered Offices: Harmondsworth, Middlesex, England

This adaptation published by Penguin Books in 1992
1 3 5 7 9 10 8 6 4 2

Text copyright © Jennifer Bassett, 1992
Illustrations copyright © Christian Birmingham, 1992
All rights reserved

The moral right of the adapter and illustrator has been asserted

Illustrations by Christian Birmingham

Printed in England by Clays Ltd, St Ives plc
Set in 11/14 pt Lasercomp Bembo

Hamlet

CHAPTER ONE

There are more things in Heaven and Earth, Horatio,
Than are dreamt of in your philosophy . . .

Act 1, Scene 5

Night, and a thin, yellow moon in the black sky. Out in the
Bristol Channel a grey fog hung over the sea, but it did not
reach the coast or climb up into the hills. There, in a small
village to the west of the city, the night was clear. Moonlight
fell among the tall stones in the **graveyard** of St Jude's
church. A breath of wind whispered through the trees. The
villagers slept, dreamt, woke, and slept again, but in the
graveyard all was still. The dead do not dream. There is only
silence in the **grave**.

A great city is never silent. There is always noise of one
kind or another – the noise of traffic and machines, of pubs
and restaurants; the noise of children crying, people laughing,
shouting, whispering . . .

Behind the walls of a factory in the south of the city, three
men waited, and watched the shadows. The tall gates in the
factory wall were locked, and the men waited in the **yard** a
little distance away. An hour passed. The moonlight grew
stronger and the shadows deeper. Then came a whisper from
one of the waiting men:

'Look! There it is! See it? It's coming straight through the
gates – just as if they weren't there! God help us!'

'It's walking away – no, it's coming back!' The second
man's eyes were wide with fear. 'It's the old man, I'm sure of

7

it. Speak to it, Horatio! You knew the old man when he was alive. Ask him why he's come back!'

The youngest of the three men stepped forward and spoke to the grey shape under the shadow of the wall. But the ghost did not answer Horatio's questions, and soon it had gone again, disappearing silently into the darkness beyond the factory walls.

The two night-watchmen were frightened and worried.

'I don't like it,' said the older man. 'When I took this job, I wasn't told about any ghosts. For two nights now, it's been walking round the factory! How can we guard a place against things that just walk straight through locked gates?'

The night-watchmen looked at Horatio, the friend of the old man's son.

'You did see it, didn't you?' the younger man asked nervously.

'Oh yes, I saw it, all right,' said Horatio slowly. 'Hamlet must be told about this,' he went on thoughtfully. 'Perhaps the ghost will speak to his own son.'

◆

At the top of the hill above the factory, a big house stood. Light streamed out from all the windows, and the sounds of laughing and talking could be heard right out in the street. The wedding party was going well.

Inside one of the large rooms at the back of the house, Claudius stood holding a glass of champagne, with one arm round his new wife, Gertrude. He had just finished telling a funny story and everybody was laughing loudly. It was not, in fact, a very funny story, but Claudius was now a very rich and **powerful** man – a **tycoon** in the business world. He was the new owner of a large group of companies, with inter-national interests in shipping, newspapers, and computers. He also owned large parts of the city, a big factory, and two hotels. His personal fortune was about twenty-five million pounds, and he was a man who never forgot an insult. So it was only sensible to laugh at his funny stories.

Hamlet did not laugh. He sat quietly in a corner, his long legs stretched out in front of him, his glass of champagne untasted in his hand. His blue eyes followed his mother, Gertrude, as she began to move around the room, laughing and talking. One or two of the girls at the party looked at Hamlet hopefully. He was easily the most handsome young man in the room, and had broken many hearts with that slow, lazy smile of his. But tonight, Hamlet did not choose to smile, and none of the girls dared to speak to him.

Eventually Gertrude came up to him. 'Do try to look a little happier, Hamlet, please. I know how sad you feel about your father, but . . . well . . . it's two months now since he died . . . and this *is* a wedding party, after all. It's not very pleasant for me or your uncle Claudius if you look like a thundercloud all the time.'

Hamlet looked up into his mother's face. 'Perhaps I feel like a thundercloud, mother,' he said.

At that moment Claudius joined them. He was a large, heavy man, with thick, iron-grey hair and a smooth face. Some people thought him handsome. He put a large, heavy hand on Hamlet's shoulder.

'Well, now,' he said, 'got a full glass, have you, boy? Good, good. I want you to enjoy yourself. Of course, it's quite natural that you're still feeling a little sad about your father's death, but it happens to us all, you know. And parents usually die before their children.' His hand was heavy on the young man's shoulder. 'But, Hamlet, I want you to think of me as your new father. Will you do that?'

Gertrude gave her son a bright smile. 'Do try to be **cheerful**, Hamlet.'

Claudius's hand was heavy on Hamlet's shoulder. 'But, Hamlet,
I want you to think of me as your new father.'

Hamlet stood up, and Claudius's hand dropped from his shoulder. 'I shall obey your every wish, mother,' he said politely.

'Excellent!' said Claudius loudly. He smiled at Hamlet, but his eyes were cold and watchful. Together, he and Gertrude moved away and joined a group of their guests.

As soon as he could, Hamlet left the room quietly and went out into the garden. It was a cool evening and none of the guests had come outside. Hamlet moved away from the house. Suddenly, with great violence, he threw his glass of champagne into a flower bed.

'To hell with them!' he said through his teeth. 'To hell with everything!'

He turned to look back at the brightly lit windows of the house, and the memories came crowding into his mind. Two months. That's all. Just two months since his father died. And his mother — all that heartbroken **sobbing**, all those tears, were now forgotten. She had married this ... this animal, this smiling snake of a man, his father's younger brother. She had taken him into her bed almost before her husband's body was cold.

His anger passed, and a deep sadness filled him. He walked slowly across the grass towards the trees at the bottom of the garden. He remembered how loving his father had been to his mother. Hamlet had been in the United States, studying business management at Harvard, when his father died. He had flown home at once, of course, and his mother had met him at the airport, her eyes red from crying. And now ... no, it was too painful to think about it. He disappeared under the trees.

There Horatio found him, sitting on a garden seat under a tall tree, which threw long moon shadows across the grass. Hamlet stood up as his friend walked towards him. 'Hi,' he said. 'I thought you'd gone home. I wouldn't blame you. It's not really your kind of party, is it? I don't think I can take any more of it myself.'

'It must be very hard for you,' said Horatio quietly.

'Oh, I don't know,' said Hamlet. He smiled brightly, showing white teeth. 'My uncle – my new father, you know – is full of kindness and wisdom. He told me that death comes to us all sooner or later. Did you know that, Horatio?' Hamlet's laugh had a sharp sound, like glass breaking.

Horatio smiled sadly. Then he put his hand on his friend's arm.

'Hamlet, I want you to come down to the factory with me,' he said carefully. 'I know you won't believe this, but . . . but I've just seen your father's ghost there. The night-watchmen saw him, too.'

Hamlet stared at him. 'My father's ghost? You're joking!' he said. But he saw pity, not amusement, in Horatio's eyes, and he knew his friend would not joke about his father's death. 'Oh my God,' he said softly. 'What did he . . .' He stopped, and pushed his hand through his long fair hair. 'OK, let's go,' he said quickly.

It was less than a mile down the hill and Hamlet's car, a long, low Lamborghini, took only a few seconds.

♦

Upstairs in the big house on the hill, a private family discussion was taking place in a small back room. Laertes was walking up and down, waving his hands around as he spoke. He was a tall, impatient young man, a few years younger than Hamlet.

'Listen, Ophelia,' he said to his sister, 'you must forget him! I'm going back to France tomorrow, to finish my studies, so I won't be around to take care of you. You're so

'Listen, Ophelia,' Laertes said to his sister, 'you must forget Hamlet! I'm going back to France tomorrow, so I won't be around to take care of you.'

young – you don't understand men! You say that Hamlet's given you presents, told you that he loves you. Well, don't believe him!'

Ophelia looked at him with her big grey eyes. 'Why shouldn't I? Are you saying he's lying?'

'Well, not lying, exactly . . . but . . . Oh, you don't understand! Hamlet's good-looking, and already very rich. He's Gertrude's only son, and Claudius is his uncle – one day Hamlet will be rich enough to buy half the country! He lives in a different world from us!'

'But Father is —' began Ophelia.

Her brother did not let her finish. 'Yes, OK, Father is Claudius's business manager, but our family isn't important enough or rich enough. Money always marries money, you know.'

'But Hamlet says money isn't important. He says he wants to marry me, and he's so kind, so gentle . . . He's not always arguing and shouting, like some people. You, for example.'

Laertes looked down into Ophelia's beautiful, heart-shaped face. He was very fond of his sister, and he knew how shy and how innocent she was. He did not want her to get hurt.

'Listen, Ophelia, just don't fall into bed with Hamlet, right? Because he won't marry you!'

Ophelia was very young. She did not like arguments and very rarely disagreed with her brother or her father.

'Perhaps you're right,' she said quietly. But her soft grey eyes were sad and full of dreams.

◆

Down at the factory they could still see the lights and hear the noise of the party in the big house on the hill. Hamlet turned his face away.

'The party will go on all night,' he told Horatio. 'Claudius

'The party will go on all night,' Hamlet told Horatio. 'Claudius
wants to make sure that all his managers and factory workers
have a good time.'

wants to make sure that all his managers and factory workers have a good time. There's enough drink in the house to make everybody sick for a week.'

One of the watchmen let them into the factory yard through a side gate. Hamlet nodded at the two watchmen, who looked at him nervously. The older man said, in a low voice, 'It's nearly midnight, sir. The ghost . . .'

'Shh! There it is now!' said Horatio quietly. 'Over there, by the wall!'

Hamlet turned and stared into the shadows. Out of the darkness a grey shape moved slowly forwards. Then it stopped. It lifted a dead, white hand, and looked at Hamlet with dead, empty eyes.

'Dear God!' Hamlet whispered. 'It *is* my father! I must speak to him.'

The ghost began to move away, still looking at Hamlet.

'It wants you to follow it,' said the younger watchman in a frightened voice. 'Don't go, sir! You don't know what might happen!'

'He's right,' Horatio said quickly. 'Stay here with us.'

He took hold of Hamlet's arm, but Hamlet pushed his hand away. 'No!' he said **fiercely**. 'I'll follow it – even if it's the **Devil** himself!' He stepped forward and began to walk across the yard. The grey shape in front of him moved away at the same speed, like a cloud of smoke blowing in the wind. But there was no wind.

At the back of the factory, where the lorries parked, the yard was in deep shadow. The moon was now low in the sky. Hamlet stopped, and put his hand flat against the wall. The feel of the rough bricks under his fingers comforted him; they were a reminder of the real world, of hard reality, where sight and sound and touch did not play tricks on the mind.

'Speak!' he said to the grey shape in front of him. His own voice sounded strange and hollow.

And out of the darkness, the ghost spoke.

'Hamlet, my son. If you feel a son's love for a father, then listen now. I haven't got much time. They told you I died peacefully in my sleep from heart failure. That was a lie, my son, a lie. I was poisoned. I died a terrible, painful death.'

'My uncle?' whispered Hamlet.

'Yes, your uncle Claudius. He stole my life, my business, and my wife. Do not harm your mother, Hamlet. But, oh my dear son, if you loved your father, then **revenge** his murder!'

The ghost's words seemed to come from a great distance, but they filled Hamlet's ears like thunder. He put his head in his hands. Had he really heard those words, or had they come from his own mind? The news did not surprise him. His uncle's smooth words and smiling face – and underneath an ugly, greedy, thieving, murdering heart! Oh no, it was no surprise to hear that Claudius had killed his father.

But now . . . what should he do now? He had loved his father dearly. The word revenge hung in his mind like a stormcloud over the sea. He took his hands away from his eyes and stared into the darkness again. There was nothing there, no voices from the shadows, no grey shape, no dead, empty eyes looking at him in pain and sadness. The factory yard was as silent and as still as death itself.

A little later, Horatio and the two watchmen saw Hamlet coming round the corner of the yard towards them. He walked as if he was drunk, with uneven steps, his face white and his hands shaking. The younger watchman hurriedly fetched an old wooden chair for Hamlet to sit on, and the three of them stood round him like visitors at a hospital bed, not knowing what to say.

Then the older watchman whispered to Horatio, 'Would

he like a drink, do you think, sir? I've got a little bottle of whisky in my bag. For the cold nights, you know.'

Hamlet heard this, and lifted his head. 'Don't say a word about this! Promise me! You've seen nothing, and you've heard nothing. Right?' His eyes were wild, dangerous.

'Yes. No. Of course, sir,' said the watchmen quickly.

Soon Hamlet and Horatio left and walked back to the car. Hamlet took his car keys out of his pocket. The colour had returned to his face now, and he spoke calmly.

'Will you drive the car back to the house for me, Horatio? I think I'll go and walk down by the river for a bit. Think things over.'

'You're sure you're all right?' asked his friend.

Hamlet laughed. He put a hand on the roof of the Lamborghini and stared up into the night sky. 'Oh yes. I'll keep a firm hold on reality. I must. If I don't, I'll go mad.' He looked at Horatio. 'You probably think I'm going mad already.'

'No, I don't,' said Horatio quietly. 'You've had a bad shock, that's all. People who see ghosts aren't always mad, you know.'

Hamlet laughed again, less wildly. 'No, I suppose not. But it's given me an idea, though. Madness, I mean.' He went on slowly. 'I might pretend to be a little mad for a time. Behave strangely. Say odd things. That might worry . . . some people. Frighten them a bit.' He turned to his friend. 'Be patient with me, Horatio. I'll tell you all about it soon. Just now I need to think. But I can see trouble coming – whichever way I look. Why, oh why, did this have to happen to me?'

CHAPTER TWO

The play's the thing,
Wherein I'll catch the conscience of the King.
Act 2, Scene 2

It was several days before people began to talk, but then the rumours travelled fast among the workers in the factory.

'Have you heard, the old man's son is sick.'

'Sick? What do you mean?'

'Sick in the head. He's gone mad! He talks strangely, walks around in a dream, and he doesn't know which day of the week it is. Our new boss, Claudius, doesn't like it at all. Very worried, he is. Thinks Hamlet could be dangerous.'

Poor Ophelia was also worried, and frightened, by Hamlet's madness. He came round to visit her one evening when Polonius was out, and was very strange indeed. Ophelia tried to talk to him, but he didn't say a word to her, just sat and looked at her. Then he held her face between his hands for a minute, shook his head sadly, and walked backwards out of the door.

Laertes was now back in France, so Ophelia was alone in the house. When her father came home, she told him all about it. She was worried about Hamlet and did not know what was the best thing to do.

Polonius was a short, fat little man, who liked to be important. He loved his daughter, of course, but he also liked to please his boss. He knew that Claudius would not be happy at a marriage between Hamlet and Ophelia. Laertes had warned his father about Hamlet before he went back to France, so Polonius had made sure that Ophelia stayed at home in the evenings. She was only seventeen, after all, and certainly not wise enough to understand the kind of games that young men like to play . . . But now, things began to look a little different.

'Well, well!' His small black eyes shone with excitement. 'Perhaps this is the answer! Perhaps he really is in love. Have you been nasty to him?'

'No. I wrote to him and told him I didn't want to see him again. But I did that because you told me to.'

'Well, I thought he was just playing around — and making a fool of you. So, has he tried to see you since then? Has he phoned you?'

'Yes,' said Ophelia miserably. 'Once. I just . . . just put the phone down. I didn't know what to say.'

'Then that's it!' said Polonius. 'It's love — he's mad with love! I'll go and see the boss tomorrow and tell him.'

♦

Claudius managed his many companies from the great house on the hill above the town. There was a big office at the top of the house, full of computers and telephones and business machines. Not long ago, of course, it had been his brother's house, and his brother's office. The 'Old Man', as the workers used to call him, in a friendly way. But they had no friendly name for the new owner. He was just the 'Boss', and he was not popular.

That Tuesday morning the two young men in Claudius's office listened carefully to what Claudius told them, and said 'Yes, sir' and 'No, sir' as often as possible. Their names were Rosencrantz and Guildenstern.

Finally, Claudius stood up, and opened his wallet. 'OK, boys,' he said. He took out two packets of bank notes. 'Find out what you can. You were good friends of his when you were all at university. Talk to him, go around with him, have a few drinks. Perhaps he's mad, and perhaps he isn't. But I want to know what's going on.'

The bank notes disappeared into the two young men's pockets. 'Thank you, sir. We'll do what we can, sir.'

Claudius smiled and put his wallet away. 'Have a word with Gertrude on your way out. She'll tell you where you're likely to find Hamlet.'

Claudius returned to his desk and his papers. There was worrying news from Scotland. Young Fortinbras in Glasgow was making trouble. He was a businessman with big ideas and a lot of money, and he wanted to use his money to buy companies in the south. Claudius's companies. And when Fortinbras wanted something, he usually got it. He already owned a large part of Claudius's computer company, which at the moment was doing good business and making a lot of money. Now he wanted to buy the rest of the company. He had the money ready and was pushing hard for a quick decision. Claudius didn't like it. There was no money in shipping at the moment, and he was having a lot of trouble with the newspapers. So he didn't want to lose the computer business. He pulled some papers towards him and began to study the figures.

◆

Later that same day the house telephone rang in Claudius's office. Polonius had arrived, his wife Gertrude told him, with some important news about Hamlet. Could Claudius come down for a minute?

Downstairs in the sitting-room, Claudius gave Polonius a glass of whisky and waited patiently for him to give his news. Polonius never used one word when he could use fifteen.

'Do get on with your story, Polonius,' said Gertrude. 'We haven't got all day to listen to you.' She was still an attractive woman, but her hair was no longer a natural colour and her face had begun to look old. She kicked off her shoes and put her legs up on the sofa. Polonius started talking about young people today and the modern way of doing things, and Gertrude's mind turned to her son. He was behaving very oddly these days. She knew he wasn't taking **drugs**, or anything silly like that. Perhaps he hadn't got enough to do? Perhaps it was time for him to get married? He was nearly thirty, after all.

Polonius was still talking, but finally Gertrude and Claudius understood what he was trying to tell them.

'So, you think that Hamlet has gone mad because he's in love with your daughter, and she's turned cold towards him – on your orders?' said Claudius.

'Yes, sir, that's it. Well, not gone mad, exactly, but he has been talking very strangely. He's known me for years, but he thought I was the postman the other day! And he's always talking about death and dying – it's difficult to make sense of it. I'm sure love is the answer, sir. I remember when I was a young man, ah yes! The pains of young love, sir, go very deep, very deep. Yes, I remember —'

Claudius turned to his wife. 'What do you think, Gertrude?'

'Perhaps,' she said slowly. She looked out of the window, down the long garden. The trees threw deep shadows across the grass in the late afternoon sunlight. 'But I think it's also his father's death and our marriage so soon afterwards.'

Polonius looked from one to the other with his little black eyes. 'I have an idea, sir – if you agree. Why don't we get them together, and secretly listen to their conversation?'

'How?' asked Claudius.

'Well, Hamlet usually spends an hour every morning reading the business pages of the newspapers in your library here, doesn't he? I'll send my daughter along tomorrow – I'll think of some excuse – and she can just walk in to the library, as if by chance. I can hide a microphone behind the books, and then you and I, sir, can listen to their conversation upstairs, in your office. Hamlet won't know anything about it.' Polonius looked hopefully at his boss.

Claudius drank his whisky and thought. 'OK,' he said. 'We'll try it. You fix it, and tell me when you're ready.'

◆

Hamlet's favourite bar was down by the river, on the edge of the city. All the windows looked out over the river. It was always comforting to watch running water, even the muddy brown waters of the river Avon.

That evening Hamlet was having a quiet drink, alone in a back room, when the door flew open and two young men appeared in the doorway, with wide smiles on their faces.

Hamlet looked up. 'Well, well, well,' he said smiling. 'If it isn't my old friends, Ros and Gilly! How are you both?'

'Oh, not bad. Up and down. You know how it is,' laughed Guildenstern.

'I certainly do,' said Hamlet. 'But what are you doing here, in this prison?'

'Prison?' said Rosencrantz. 'What do you mean, Hamlet?'

'This city's a prison, Ros. One of the worst. Didn't you know?'

'Oh, come on, Hamlet! Bristol's a great place,' said Rosencrantz.

'And you've got everything you want here,' added Guildenstern.

Hamlet looked at his two friends. 'But tell me,' he said, 'why have you come?' He was still smiling, but the smile did not reach his eyes.

'Just to see you, have a few drinks, you know,' said Guildenstern.

'Naturally, I'm delighted to see you,' said Hamlet smoothly. 'But let's be honest, shall we? You didn't come by chance — you were sent for. Claudius and Gertrude sent for you, right?'

Rosencrantz looked a little confused. 'Why should they send for us?' he laughed.

'*You* tell *me*,' said Hamlet, watching him. There was a pause. 'Come on, now. We're old friends, aren't we?'

Rosencrantz and Guildenstern looked at each other, embarrassed, and then into Hamlet's cold blue eyes.

'Yeah, OK. We were sent for,' said Rosencrantz slowly.

Hamlet put his feet up on a chair, and drank some more of his beer. 'And I'll tell you why,' he said. 'Then you won't have to lie to Claudius.' His voice became low and serious. 'Just recently, the world has seemed very black to me — a **miserable**, cruel, dirty place, without hope or promise. I can't get any enjoyment out of life, and I've lost interest in women. Why do you smile?' he finished fiercely.

'I was just thinking,' said Guildenstern quickly, 'that if you're in that kind of mood, the student theatre group won't get much of a welcome from you! We heard that they're coming here to put on a play for the workers in your uncle's factory.'

Hamlet put down his beer glass. 'Which student theatre group?' he asked.

'The ones we knew at university. You used to like them a lot,' said Rosencrantz. 'They're staying at your uncle's hotel near the factory.'

'Yes, I remember them,' Hamlet said thoughtfully. 'I'll be very glad to see them — very glad.' He stood up and picked up his empty beer glass. 'But my uncle-father and my aunt-mother are wrong, you know.'

'Wrong about what, Hamlet?' said Rosencrantz carefully.

Rosencrantz and Guildenstern looked at each other in embarrassed silence.

Hamlet smiled kindly at them. 'I'm only mad on Tuesdays. The rest of the week I know exactly what's going on.' He looked amused at his friends' embarrassment. 'Come on. Let's go down to the bar. I'll buy you a few beers, and you can tell me all the news from London – who's sleeping with who, who's losing money, who's making it . . .'

♦

At the White Horse Hotel later that night, a group of people sat round a table in an upstairs room. They drank their beer and listened carefully to a young man with long fair hair and brilliant blue eyes.

'When you do your play at my uncle's factory tomorrow night, I'd like you to do *The Murder of Gonzago*. Can you?'

'Sure. We can do that,' said the first actor, an older man with a great black beard and moustache.

'And I'd like to put in a few lines of my own at the beginning of the play. If I write them tonight, and bring them to you early tomorrow morning, could you learn them by the evening?'

'No problem,' said the first actor.

Hamlet smiled. 'Great! Now it's a thirsty business, acting. Let me buy you all some more beer.'

The drinking went on for some time. The theatre group travelled all round the country, putting on plays in churches, factories, back rooms in pubs. Its members did not make much money, but they certainly knew how to enjoy themselves. Jokes flew around the room and the stories got wilder and wilder. Hamlet listened in amusement, and paid for the beer.

One of the younger actors, a Welshman with red hair, had an endless memory for stories.

'Have you heard this one?' he asked and went on without

waiting for an answer. 'There was this one-legged man who lived with his aunt in a house in Fulham . . .'

Hamlet had heard the story before and he stopped listening. For the hundredth time his thoughts returned to his problem, going round and round, like a rat caught in a wheel. Murder. If you loved your father, then revenge his murder. There were no witnesses to the crime; neither the police nor the law could help him. No one would believe a story of murder. Why should they? It had looked like a natural death. Doctors had examined the body, signed the correct forms; there were no unanswered questions. Only two people alive knew what had really happened, himself and Claudius – the murderer. *If you loved your father, then revenge his murder.*

' . . . Then he went out and bought a ladder, six eggs, half a kilo of sugar, and a woolly hat . . .'

Revenge. An eye for an eye, a tooth for a tooth, a death for a death. Another murder. Against the laws of God and Man. How could he murder another human being? And then he would probably spend the rest of his life in prison. But what other way was there? How could he ever sleep again, with the memory of the ghost's words and the ghost's dead eyes?

' . . . So he sold it for a thousand pounds and his aunt never spoke to him again!'

There was a burst of laughter, and the man with the black beard said, 'Oh God, that's terrible!' He turned to Hamlet and put a friendly hand on his shoulder. 'You OK, Hamlet?' he said kindly.

'Yeah. Sure. It's good to see you all again. Reminds me of the old days in London.' Hamlet smiled his slow, lazy smile, and the man with the black beard nodded and turned back to his friends. Another story had begun.

His father's ghost. Had he really heard those words, seen

His father's ghost. Had he really heard those words, seen those eyes? Could the mind play a trick like that?

those eyes? Could the mind play a trick like that? First, he must make sure. With a few changes, *The Murder of Gonzago* was very similar to the story of his father's murder. He would make Claudius go and see the play. Surely that would bring the shame, the guilt, to that smooth face and those cold, smiling eyes?

CHAPTER THREE

> *To be, or not to be – that is the question . . .*
> *To die, to sleep –*
> *To sleep – perchance to dream. Ay, there's the rub . . .*
>   Act 3, Scene 1

At nine o'clock on Wednesday morning Polonius hurried up the steps to the front door of the big house on the hill. It was a grey day, with a cool wind blowing up the river from the sea. Polonius looked at his watch. He had a busy day in front of him – arrangements to make, meetings to go to, letters to write. He hurried inside and up the stairs.

There were already several people in the office on the top floor. Claudius nodded to Polonius as he came in, then turned back to Rosencrantz and Guildenstern.

'So you have no idea what's on his mind?' he said thoughtfully.

'No, sir,' said Guildenstern. 'Sorry. He just wouldn't tell us.'

'But was he glad to see you?' asked Gertrude. 'Is he a bit more cheerful now, do you think?'

'Oh yes,' Rosencrantz said quickly. 'I think we made him feel more cheerful. And he's very enthusiastic about this theatre group and the play at the factory tonight. You will go and see it, won't you? Hamlet very much wants you both to go.' He looked hopefully at Gertrude and then at Claudius.

'Of course,' Claudius said. 'I'm looking forward to it. I've heard these actors are very good.' He saw Polonius nodding at him and looking at the clock on the wall. He turned to Gertrude. 'My love, why don't you take these young men off for a cup of coffee? I've got some business to arrange with Polonius.'

As soon as they had left, Polonius told Claudius that he had fixed the meeting between his daughter and Hamlet. 'It's all ready, sir. Hamlet's in the library as usual, and Ophelia will be here at ten. I've checked the microphone's working, so we'll be able to hear everything they say.'

The subject of all this interest was sitting in the library at the back of the house. The morning newspapers lay on a desk in front of him. Hamlet had finished reading the business pages and was now looking at the rest of the news. There seemed to be a lot about death. NINE DIE IN MOTORWAY ACCIDENT. Stupid, senseless deaths. JEALOUS HUSBAND KILLS WIFE WITH MEAT KNIFE. An ugly, horrible murder. The man was probably mad. Hamlet did not read the story. YOUNG GIRL THROWS HERSELF UNDER TRAIN. What a terrible way to die – to be torn to pieces by metal wheels. Why had she done it? He read her story. She had certainly had an unhappy life, and now she had escaped from all her worries and problems. She had found peace.

Or had she? Hamlet stared at the rows of books on the wall. He had read most of them, but none of them had the answer to that question. Perhaps many people would choose to die, to escape from their miserable little lives, if they were sure of finding peace. But no one knew what that long sleep, death, would bring. Maybe it was better to stay with the misery you knew. Perhaps beyond the grave there were unimaginable **horrors**. His mind turned to the graveyard of St Jude's church, where his father was **buried** . . .

◆

Ophelia walked slowly up the steps to the front door. She felt sick with fear. Why did she have to do this? Her father was using her like a tool, to please his boss. He never stopped talking long enough to listen to her. When he had finished using her, perhaps he would throw her away, put her out with the rubbish one Monday morning.

Only one person had ever listened to her, had cared about her feelings, had not laughed at her ideas. But she no longer knew what Hamlet thought or felt. Perhaps she had never known.

There was nobody around on the stairs at the back of the house. She walked into the library as quietly as a mouse, and stood still, staring at Hamlet's back. After a few seconds he lifted his head and looked at her.

'Ophelia.' His blue eyes were cool and watchful.

Ophelia took a deep breath. 'How are you, Hamlet? I just came to, um, return some magazines to your mother, and she said that you were in here, and I thought . . . um, well, I've been wanting to give you back your ring, you see, and I thought . . .' Why didn't he say something? Tell her to go away, jump in a river. It was obvious that he didn't want to talk to her. He had probably never been in love with her at all.

Hamlet stood up and came towards her. She moved back against the wall, nervously. She must try to sound natural, unworried.

'I never gave you any rings, Ophelia,' he said gently.

'But you did.' She looked up at him, confused. 'This little gold one. You've probably forgotten all about it.' She pulled it off her little finger and held it out to him. 'I don't think I ought to keep it, now . . . now that . . .'

He was standing very close to her. She swallowed, and fixed her eyes on his shirt. It was a lovely soft creamy colour. Whatever happened, she must not cry. She felt his fingers on her cheek, in her hair. She closed her eyes.

'I loved you, Ophelia,' he said quietly, 'not so very long ago.'

'You made me believe that you did,' she whispered.

'Perhaps that was foolish of you.' His fingers moved gently through her hair, and she felt his warm breath on her face. She kept very still. 'I never loved you,' he said softly.

'Then it certainly was foolish of me to believe you.' Tears burned at the back of her eyes.

He took her chin in his hand and lifted her face towards his own. His voice became fierce and angry. 'You must never get married, Ophelia, do you hear me? All men are cruel and false. Don't believe any of them. Go home and sleep alone, in your own bed. Where's your father?'

Ophelia's big grey eyes stared up into his face. 'At . . . at his office.'

'Then tell him to stay there, and not to play games with other people's lives.'

Suddenly, he let her go, and began to walk fiercely round the room, knocking books and newspapers on to the floor and staring up at the walls and ceiling. Ophelia put her shaking hands behind her back. She had never seen Hamlet like this before. The last, small hope in her heart died, and she felt more lonely than she had ever felt in her life.

'Go home and stay there! All women are false too. There's not an innocent one among you.' He was shouting now. 'We won't have any more marriages. Oh no! Those who are married already can go on living – all except one. But we won't have any more!'

His fingers moved gently through her hair, and she felt his warm breath on her face. She kept very still. 'I never loved you,' he said softly.

Upstairs in the office, Claudius looked very thoughtful. Through the microphone they had heard the crash of the library door closing, and after that there were no more voices. Only the sound of quiet sobbing.

'Well, he's clearly not in love. But there's certainly something on his mind, all right. And I'd like to know what it is. He could become dangerous.' Claudius turned a gold pen over and over in his fingers.

'Perhaps his mother can get him to talk. I've got another idea,' said Polonius quickly. 'Tonight, after the play, your wife could take Hamlet back to her private sitting-room for a little talk. I could hide behind those long curtains at the window, and listen.'

'OK. Let's try that. But perhaps Hamlet should go away for a time. I think I'll send him to Canada. I've got some good friends there, who'll take care of him for me.'

◆

At one end of the big factory building there was a large room, which the workers used for their meetings. It was not a theatre, of course, but the travelling actors preferred ordinary rooms. They liked to bring their plays right into the middle of people's lives. They saw no difference between the theatre and the real world; one was a mirror for the other.

The Murder of Gonzago was an old, but still popular, play – about a king and a queen in far-away Italy. The story was not very complicated. The king's brother killed the king, then took the kingdom and married the queen. There was a prince as well, of course, who was the son of the murdered king. It was all good entertainment, about murder, death, and revenge. Tonight, the king's brother was going to use poison for his murder, not a knife.

Hamlet had written the lines about the poison during Tuesday night and taken them round to the White Horse very early that morning. The Welshman with the red hair, who was acting the king's brother, liked the new lines very much. 'Nasty,' he had said, 'but very clever.'

By eight o'clock that evening the room was nearly full. People were rushing around, squeezing in extra chairs at the back for the late-comers. The actor with the black beard was very pleased. 'All tickets sold,' he said to Hamlet. 'We'll make a bit of money tonight.'

Hamlet smiled, and turned to Horatio. 'Claudius will be over there,' he said quietly, pointing to the other side of the room. 'I want you to watch his face, like a cat at a mouse-hole. I'm sure his guilt will show, when he hears the lines I've written.'

'Don't worry,' said his friend calmly. 'If even his left eyebrow moves, I'll see it.'

'Where would I be without you, Horatio?' said Hamlet, smiling sadly. 'You've got more common sense and more wisdom than anyone I know. Your intelligence and your feelings never pull you in two different directions at the same time. Not like me.'

As he spoke, Polonius hurried past them, with some programmes in his hand. 'Good to see you looking a bit happier, Hamlet,' he called out.

'I'm as happy as a postman in the rain,' replied Hamlet, with a bright, fixed smile.

'Oh, you and your jokes, Hamlet!' Polonius laughed, and hurried on.

'Silly old fool,' said Hamlet quietly to himself.

Claudius and Gertrude now arrived and took their seats. Horatio moved quietly to his seat in the corner, and Hamlet went to sit next to Ophelia in the front row.

Ophelia had not wanted to come to the play, but her father had told her not to be so silly. She sat, stiff and straight on her chair, and did not look at the handsome face by her side. Nobody knew about the black misery in her heart, and she certainly wasn't going to let Hamlet see it. Oh no. She was too proud to do that.

Hamlet put his arm along the back of her chair, and looked at her. Ophelia looked down at her programme. Oh, why didn't the play begin? The minutes seemed endless. One of them had to say something, surely? She turned the pages of her programme.

'The play only lasts an hour. It's very short.'

'As short as a woman's love,' said Hamlet, pleasantly. His eyes followed the soft lines of her neck.

Ophelia lifted her chin higher and swallowed nervously. She did not turn to look at him. 'Very amusing,' she said coolly.

At last, the lights went out and the play began.

The Welshman was a fine actor. He looked like a devil out of hell, dancing with delight and waving his little bottle of poison in the air. His eyes shone with a mad light, and his words whispered round the room like a snake's tongue.

When the King's brother poured the poison into the sleeping King's ear, Claudius suddenly stood up. His chair crashed to the floor behind him.

'I'm not sitting through this rubbish!' he shouted, his face purple with anger. He turned and pushed his way out of the room.

Immediately, there was noise and confusion. Gertrude and Polonius hurried after Claudius. The lights came on, and people began talking in loud surprise.

Hamlet and Horatio went outside quickly, into the factory yard. Hamlet hit his friend on the shoulder in his excitement.

'I'm not sitting through this rubbish!' Claudius shouted, his face
purple with anger.

'Did you see that, Horatio! My God! I'll take the ghost's word for a thousand pounds!'

'Throwing money away,' said Horatio with a half-smile. 'A hundred would be enough.'

Hamlet laughed, then turned quickly at the sound of running footsteps behind them. It was Guildenstern, with Rosencrantz right behind him.

'Hamlet!' said Guildenstern breathlessly. 'Claudius is really unhappy.'

'Got a pain in his stomach, has he?' said Hamlet brightly.

'He's angry, Hamlet. Very angry. And your mother wants to see you at once, up at the house. She asked us to tell you.'

'Ah, my mother's orders, eh? I'll come when I'm ready. Not before.'

'Why don't you tell us what's worrying you, Hamlet?' asked Rosencrantz urgently. 'We're old friends. I'm sure we can help.'

'Why does the Earth go round the Sun, Ros? And the Moon go round the Earth?'

'What? I've no idea, Hamlet, but why —'

'Come on now. Think about it! Try!'

'But I'm not a scientist – I don't know the answer.'

Hamlet stared at him with cold blue eyes. 'Then you could never understand my problem, Ros. It's too complicated for your little brain.'

◆

Claudius finished his third cup of coffee. His voice was calm, controlled.

'Yes,' he said, 'a change of air will do him good. Canada's a wonderful place. Lots to do and see. It'll give him something new to think about.'

'I'm sure you're right, sir,' said Rosencrantz.

'I'm very grateful to you two boys. You've given me a lot of your time. I won't forget that.'

'It's no trouble, sir, none at all,' Guildenstern said. 'And we're delighted to go off to Canada. We'll keep an eye on him for you, sir.'

'I've got a business to manage, boys. You know that. I really haven't got time to worry about this crazy son of Gertrude's.' Claudius stood up. 'OK. The flight's at five o'clock tomorrow morning. Bristol–London–Toronto. The tickets will be at the desk in Bristol airport. I'll tell Hamlet about it myself, later tonight, after he's seen his mother.'

At that moment Polonius burst into the room. 'Sir, he's here! I've just seen his car arrive. I'll run down to his mother's room and hide. Afterwards I'll come straight up here, sir, and tell you what I've heard.'

'Thanks, Polonius. I'm grateful for your help.'

The little man hurried out busily, and the two young men followed him. Claudius poured himself a large whisky and took it over to the window. Down below he could see Hamlet's red Lamborghini parked in front of the house.

The murder of a brother. Cain and Abel. The first, and the oldest crime. He would never be free of the guilt. He would have to live with it. But he had got the money, and the power, and the woman that he had wanted. And her son. Claudius drank a little whisky. What *did* Hamlet know? Was he guessing . . . or did he actually know? But how, in God's name, *could* he know?

♦

Gertrude's private sitting-room was next to the guest bed-rooms on the ground floor. It was an attractive, restful room, with beautiful Chinese wallpaper and carpets in soft colours. There were many valuable works of art in the room, mostly paintings and small **statues** from Eastern countries. Long windows opened out onto a rose garden at the side of the house. Tonight the windows were closed, and the long curtains shut out the night.

From behind the curtains Polonius spoke. 'You mustn't be too soft with him, you know. Claudius is getting very annoyed. There'll be trouble soon, and none of us wants that.'

'I know, I know,' said Gertrude impatiently. 'I'll do my best . . . Shh . . . He's coming.' She sat down on a sofa with her back to the light.

The door opened. Hamlet came in, closed the door quietly behind him, and walked across to his mother. There was a fierce light in his brilliant blue eyes, and his voice was hard and cold. There was no doubt in his mind now about the ghost's words, and later tonight he would take the law into his own hands, find his uncle, and . . . Oh yes. But first, his mother.

'Now, mother, what's the matter?'

'Hamlet, you've made your father very unhappy.'

'Mother, you've made *my* father very unhappy.'

'Don't try to be clever with me, Hamlet. Have you forgotten who I am?'

'No. How could I? You're your husband's brother's wife . . . and, unfortunately, also my mother.'

Gertrude stood up. 'If you're going to insult me, Hamlet, I'll —'

'Oh no.' Hamlet's strong hand was around her wrist. 'Sit down, mother, and listen to me. I have something to tell you.'

The look in those ice-cold eyes frightened Gertrude. She tried to pull her wrist away. 'Let go, Hamlet, you're hurting me!'

There was a sudden movement behind the curtain, and

Hamlet turned his head sharply. 'What the hell's that?' His fingers dug into Gertrude's wrist and his eyes burned in a face she did not recognize. 'It's Claudius, isn't it?' he shouted at her.

Without waiting for an answer, he pushed her violently to one side. Then in one lightning movement he **seized** from a table behind him a small, heavy, gold statue and threw himself towards the window like a cat. There was a terrible, sickening sound as the heavy gold statue crashed down on the head of the body behind the curtain. Hamlet stepped back and, slowly, the body fell to the floor, pulling the curtain down with it.

Gertrude stared in horror. Her face was grey and her hands were pressed tightly together. 'Oh my God!' she whispered. 'What have you done?'

Hamlet bent down and pulled the curtain away. The body lay still, the eyes open and already fixed in death. Hamlet stood like a man turned to stone. Seconds passed. 'You silly, foolish old man,' he said at last, in a low voice. 'I thought you were Claudius. Why, oh why, couldn't you keep out of this? God knows, I didn't want you to die.'

Gertrude pressed her hand to her mouth, trying hard not to scream. 'Oh Hamlet,' she whispered, 'why do you hate your uncle so much?'

'Because, dear mother, he murdered my father.' Hamlet bent down, picked up the small, heavy, gold statue and carefully put it back on the table. His face was white, and his mouth a thin hard line across his face.

'Murdered?' Gertrude's legs were shaking so much that she could not stand. Weakly, she felt for the sofa with her hands and sat down.

'Yes. Murdered. And you, dear mother, couldn't wait to climb into the murderer's bed, could you? Did you have no shame? No pity? No real sadness for the kind, honest man who had loved you so much, for so many years? Were you blind? Couldn't you see what kind of a man my uncle was? A selfish, greedy, cowardly, murdering thief?'

Gertrude covered her face with her hands. 'Don't, please, don't go on, Hamlet.' She began to sob quietly. 'Oh, Hamlet, why have you told me? You'll break my heart.'

He bent over the back of the sofa and held his mother's shoulders with hard, angry hands. He put his mouth close to her ear.

'How could you let that animal touch your body, mother? Kissing you, and holding you with his dirty hands. Aren't you ashamed,' he whispered fiercely, 'at your age, to behave like some sex-mad girl?'

'Oh, Hamlet, stop . . . please stop . . .' Her face was wet with tears.

Hamlet straightened and stared down at her. Then he heard a ghostly voice in his mind. *Do not harm your mother, Hamlet.* Slowly, his anger turned to pity. He went down on his knees and took Gertrude's hands in his own. The ghost's words were still ringing in his ears and for a second he closed his eyes and shook his head, trying to clear his mind.

Gertrude stared at him in fear. 'What is it, Hamlet?' she whispered.

'I'm not mad, mother,' he said tiredly. 'Don't try to comfort yourself that way.' He lifted his head and looked into her eyes. 'We can't undo the past, mother. But don't sleep with my uncle again. And say nothing to him.'

'I'll never say a word to any living person. Oh, Hamlet, Hamlet!' She began to sob again, hopelessly.

He held her hands tightly. 'It's all right, mother. It's all right.'

But it was not all right. And it never would be again.

'How could you let that animal touch your body, mother? Kissing
you, and holding you,' he whispered fiercely.

CHAPTER FOUR

I do not know
Why yet I live to say 'This thing's to do',
Since I have cause, and will, and strength, and means
To do it.

Act 4, Scene 4

There was no sleep for anyone in the big house that night. Hamlet pulled the dead body of Polonius out of his mother's sitting-room and hid it. Gertrude went to tell Claudius the terrible news, and asked him to help her poor, crazy boy. He was her only son, she said, with tears running down her face. He had **attacked** Polonius in a wild, mad anger, and he was deeply sorry now for what he had done.

Claudius began to know real fear. That violent attack had surely been intended for him. Next time . . . no, there would not be a next time. He must make sure of that. He started to make plans. He phoned his private secretary, Osric, and asked him to come urgently to the office. He paid Osric a lot of money to do exactly what he was told, and to keep his mouth shut. Then he sent for Rosencrantz and Guildenstern, and told them to find Hamlet, and Polonius's body, at once.

They found Hamlet in the kitchen, with his feet on the table, drinking coffee and watching an old American film on the television. Shocked, Guildenstern turned the television off.

'I was watching that,' said Hamlet, annoyed.

'Hamlet,' Rosencrantz said urgently, 'what have you done with the body?'

Hamlet looked at his watch. 'Eleven o'clock. You're working late tonight, Ros. I hope Claudius is paying you well.'

'I don't understand you, Hamlet. I think you've gone completely mad.'

'Claudius wants to see you,' said Guildenstern. 'Come on.'

Across the desk Hamlet met his uncle's eyes calmly. Claudius stared back at him heavily.

'Now, Hamlet, where's Polonius?'

Hamlet smiled brilliantly. 'In heaven. Send somebody there to look for him. If they don't find him, then you can go to hell . . . and look for him yourself.'

There was a thunderous silence. Rosencrantz coughed nervously.

'Hamlet,' said Claudius slowly, through his teeth, 'where – is – Polonius?'

Hamlet gave an enormous yawn, and put his hand politely over his mouth. 'Well, if you don't find him in the next week, you'll smell him as you go past the door of the blue bedroom on the ground floor.'

Claudius nodded to Osric, who quickly left the office. Claudius turned back to Hamlet.

'Listen carefully. Your mother's deeply unhappy about all this. Because of that, I won't call in the police. I'll do my best to **cover up** this . . . this unfortunate killing. Money can usually buy silence. But clearly, you must leave the country at once. Tonight. Rosencrantz and Guildenstern – who are still good friends of yours, although I don't know why – will take you to Canada. I know some people there, who'll keep you out of trouble. Your flight leaves at five o'clock.'

'So,' said Hamlet pleasantly, 'you'll cover up the old man's death. Because of my mother. How kind you are . . . father. How very kind.'

He turned his back on Claudius and put a friendly hand on Guildenstern's shoulder. 'Well, boys, off to Canada, are we? What fun!'

Hamlet put a friendly hand on Guildenstern's shoulder. 'Well, boys, off to Canada, are we? What fun!'

When they had all left the room, Claudius began to feel safer. He hoped, with all his heart, that he would never see Hamlet again. He had some good friends in Canada, very good friends. He had helped them in the past, and now they would help him. They were very good at arranging 'accidents'. In a few days' time, Claudius hoped, he would have to tell Gertrude the sad news of her son's unfortunate death.

♦

Hamlet drove north up the motorway at a hundred and twenty miles an hour. The Lamborghini ate up the miles greedily – its smooth, powerful engine was no more than a whisper in the dark wet night. Hamlet had packed his bags, and told Ros and Gilly that he needed to be alone. He would meet them at Bristol airport at four o'clock. They had tried to stop him going for a drive, but he had just walked away.

He felt sick and confused. *If you loved your father, then revenge his murder.* He thought he had done it. Blood everywhere. Blood calling for blood. But no. A mistake. A terrible, horrible mistake. And now he had to run away, and leave his uncle to cover up for him. What a mess . . . What an awful, crazy, bloody mess. A hundred and forty. He realized he was driving too fast on the wet road. He slowed down, moved over to the side of the motorway and stopped. The rain was suddenly loud on the roof of the car.

He came out of his dark dreams to see the blue light of a police car, which had just pulled up behind him. The driver got out and walked up to the Lamborghini. Hamlet opened his window.

'Everything OK, sir?' asked the policeman.

'Yes. I was just feeling a bit sleepy. Stopped for a few minutes' rest.'

The policeman bent down and looked closely at Hamlet's face.

'It's all right, officer,' said Hamlet calmly. 'I haven't been drinking.'

'Good. Glad to hear it,' the policeman said politely. He straightened up and looked at the long, powerful body of the Lamborghini. His eyes came back to Hamlet's face.

'Well, good-night, sir. Drive carefully now.'

Hamlet started the engine and drove away, at a sensible speed, into the night. Go carefully. Yes. Go to your uncle's house. Go like a thief in the dead of the night. Go on ghostly feet to his room. Go with a long bright knife in your hand and drive it into his black, guilty heart. Yes. Go carefully.

But first he must go to Canada, with his two old friends, Ros and Gilly. His prison guards. There was a pair of poisonous little snakes for you. He wondered what orders Claudius had given them. How much did an 'accidental' death cost these days? Was that what was waiting for him in Canada? He would have to play a dangerous little game with Ros and Gilly. But he would win it. Oh yes.

Soon he turned and drove south again. Revenge. He knew now, without a shadow of doubt, that his uncle was guilty. How soon could he come back to England? Not until Polonius, poor old fool, was officially dead and lawfully buried, and Claudius had paid the right people to keep quiet. Polonius. Ophelia's father. Oh God, what had he done? How many more lives was he going to wreck before his father's ghost was satisfied?

◆

On Friday morning Gertrude sat in the big sitting-room, turning the pages of a magazine. It contained a lot of practical advice on how older women could look younger, but Gertrude did not read it. Not even the latest fashions in clothes interested her. As she sat there, she heard a light knock on the door, and her housekeeper came into the room.

'Could you come out to the hall for a minute, ma'am? I've just met Polonius's daughter, Ophelia, in the street and brought her back here. I think you ought to have a look at her.'

'I'm busy,' said Gertrude.

'I don't think she's very well. She's behaving very strangely.' The woman lowered her voice. 'I think it's drugs.'

Gertrude got up and went out into the hall. Ophelia was sitting quietly on a chair by the wall. Her eyes were wide and empty, and she stared at Gertrude without recognition. Then she held up her hands in front of her face.

'I can see the bones through my skin,' she said conversationally. 'They're a sort of blue-green colour, like the sea. And they bend, like plastic. My father's bones were all purple, all the way through . . . Did you know that?' She turned her empty grey eyes towards the housekeeper. 'His bones have gone to the butcher's now, for the dogs to eat.'

'Poor child, poor child!' said Gertrude softly. 'She was terribly shocked by her father's sudden death.'

'I've heard there are several places in the town where you can get drugs, if you know who to ask,' said the housekeeper. 'It's cruel, it really is . . . a young girl like this. Shall I call the doctor?'

'Yes. I know he gave her some kind of drug to calm her down after she heard the news about her father. Perhaps she's taken too much of that. Take her to one of the guest rooms for the moment. I'll go and tell my husband.'

The housekeeper took Ophelia's hand and led her away. Slowly, Gertrude climbed the stairs to Claudius's office. She found him staring moodily out of the window. He listened in silence to her news, then shook his head.

'Oh Gertrude, troubles never come alone, do they? It's just one disaster after another. I've got so many things to worry about.' He pushed some papers around on his desk. 'There's your crazy son, and poor old Polonius, who was buried in a great hurry yesterday. That's cost me a small fortune, I can tell you. And money's a big problem at the moment. That greedy little Scotsman, Fortinbras, is trying to squeeze me out of my own companies. He wants to buy everything I own. And today, my bank manager has started asking a lot of difficult questions. Polonius used to take care of all that – he was very good at it. I didn't have any trouble with the bank when he was around.'

He turned to Gertrude. 'And then there's Laertes, too. What's he going to say when he hears about his father? That's another worry.'

They soon found out. Laertes was a popular young man, with many friends in the city. One of them had phoned him in Paris and told him there was something rather strange about his father's sudden death. Laertes arrived at the big house on the hill while Claudius and Gertrude were having lunch that day. He burst in like the north wind, shouting about murder and revenge and lying, cowardly lawyers. It was a long time before he was calm enough to listen to them. At last, Claudius was able to explain that Polonius had died in a terrible accident, after being attacked by a madman. The madman had not known what he was doing.

Laertes was not satisfied. 'But why isn't this madman in prison? Or locked up in a hospital?'

Gertrude turned her face away. 'It was my son,' she whispered. 'Hamlet. We've sent him abroad.' Bravely, she turned back to Laertes. 'And there's another thing you have to know. Come with me.'

They took him to the room where Ophelia was. Laertes stared in shock and horror at his changed sister. She did not know who he was. She sat on the edge of the bed, smiling

Laertes stared in shock and horror at his changed sister. She sat on the edge of the bed, smiling crazily at nothing.

crazily at nothing. Laertes took her hands, but she pulled them quickly away.

'Mustn't touch,' she whispered, looking at him with big round eyes. 'Oh no, no, no. Don't believe any of them. Stay at home. No touching, no kissing, no holding hands . . . My father's in a wooden box now.' She gave a little, meaningless laugh. 'Wooden box, wooden box . . .'

Laertes looked helplessly at Gertrude. 'How long has she been like this?'

'We don't know,' said Gertrude. 'We think it could be drugs, but we don't know what drug she's taken, or where she got it from. The doctor says he can't do anything for her at the moment. We must wait until the effects of the drug have passed.'

'It's my father's death, isn't it?' said Laertes angrily. 'That's why she's like this. It's the shock, it's too much for her.'

Claudius put a comforting arm round the young man's shoulders. 'Come up to my office for a minute. We'll have a talk about it.'

◆

Horatio studied the envelope that he had just found inside his front door. A telegram from Canada. From Hamlet. Quickly, he tore it open. The message was short. PLEASE BRING CAR TO LONDON HEATHROW TO MEET FLIGHT BA 723 AT 1400 HOURS NEXT SATURDAY. HAMLET. What had happened out there? Horatio wondered. Why was he coming back so soon?

The first question was also going through Claudius's mind. But why was he coming back at all? The plan had gone badly wrong. The message on Claudius's telegram was very different. CANADA IS BEAUTIFUL BUT BORING, DEAR FATHER. COMING HOME SATURDAY. LOOKING FORWARD VERY MUCH TO SEEING YOU. HAMLET.

This son of Gertrude's, Claudius thought, was like a deadly insect that would not leave him alone. He *must* get rid of him. Silently, he passed the telegram to Laertes. It had arrived soon after he and Laertes had begun their little talk in the office.

Laertes read it and looked up. 'But you just told me that Hamlet was never coming back to this country.'

'That's what I thought. Hoped.'

Laertes stared at him. 'I don't believe Hamlet's mad.'

'No,' said Claudius calmly. 'He probably isn't.'

Laertes narrowed his eyes. 'Why didn't you bring in the police? Why did you cover up my father's death?' His voice was getting louder.

Claudius shook his head sadly. 'You're right to ask me that, Laertes. Perhaps I was wrong. But Gertrude, you know, is very, very fond of her son. It would break her heart to see him in prison.'

'But Polonius was my father – and Hamlet killed him! I'm going to call in the police!'

'That would make life quite difficult for me now, wouldn't it? Listen, Laertes. I am deeply unhappy about your father's death, believe me. He was a wonderful manager. In my company I need people like him . . . and you. I'm sure you remember, Laertes, that there's an excellent job waiting for you here. The kind of opportunity that every young man hopes for.'

There was a long pause. 'Perhaps we don't need to call in the law,' said Laertes. There was another silence. 'But I still want revenge for my father's death!'

'Of course you do,' agreed Claudius smoothly. 'Very natural in a young man.' He put his elbows on the desk and rested his chin on his hands . . . and waited.

Laertes stood up and began to walk around the room. 'I was very fond of my father. He was a silly old fool sometimes

– but he was my father! And now my sister . . . Maybe it's the shock, maybe it's drugs, I don't know. But she's a sweet, gentle girl, and this shock might damage her for the rest of her life. She was in love with Hamlet, you know. I warned her, but she thought the sun shone out of his eyes. He killed my father and he's broken my sister's heart!' Laertes stopped and stared at Claudius. 'Is he going to come back to this country, and walk around a free man, laughing in my face?'

'Do you really want revenge, or do you just want to talk about it?' asked Claudius, looking bored.

The answer came back like a gunshot. 'I'd cut his throat with a blunt kitchen knife in the middle of a crowded street in daylight!'

Claudius smiled. He had found the tool, the instrument for murder, that he wanted. This violent young man was a natural killer.

'Well, that's certainly enthusiastic, but perhaps not very sensible. You don't want to spend the rest of your life in prison, do you?'

Laertes pulled a chair up to the desk and sat down. 'You'd be glad to see him in his grave too, wouldn't you? So how do we do it?'

The plan was soon made. It must look, of course, as if Hamlet had killed himself. Many people already believed that Hamlet had become very strange because of his father's death. It would be easy to spread more rumours about his madness – a madness that had driven the poor young man to kill himself. But first, Claudius would arrange a secret meeting – a **reconciliation** between the two young men, when they would forgive and forget. They would drink to the reconciliation with the very best champagne – with something special in Hamlet's glass. Some kind of drug to make him sleepy, and unable to fight back, Claudius said. He knew where he could get hold of a drug like that. Then, Laertes could attack Hamlet safely, and knock him **unconscious**. Gertrude would be kept out of this meeting, of course. Later, Hamlet's unconscious body would be carried out to the Lamborghini, and somewhere on a lonely road that night by the Bristol Channel, the car would drive off the road and crash down into the sea below, killing the driver immediately.

They were still working on the details when the door opened and Gertrude came in. Her face was white.

'Oh Laertes! The most terrible news! The police have just phoned. Ophelia . . . She seemed calmer this afternoon, and she told my housekeeper she was going home. But . . . but she didn't go home . . . She went down into the town and . . .' Gertrude's voice shook as she went on. 'Oh Laertes, she threw herself off the bridge into the river. Two boys saw her and ran for help, and a police boat reached her and pulled her out. They tried to start her breathing again, but . . . it was too late. She was already dead, Laertes.'

Tears do not come easily to young men. Their feelings show themselves in other ways. Laertes' voice was tight and hard.

'I'll kill him! I'll kill him with my own hands!'

CHAPTER FIVE

If it be now, 'tis not to come. If it be not to come,
it will be now. If it be not now, yet it will come.
The readiness is all.

Act 5, Scene 2

The church of St Jude's stands on a hill above the village. From the graveyard you can see the great city of Bristol to the east. But the noise of the city does not travel this far; the graveyard is a peaceful place. That afternoon, though, it was not quite so peaceful. There were sounds of digging, and a rough male voice singing a cheerful little song.

Near the west wall of the graveyard, under some trees, Hamlet stood by his father's grave, looking down at the gravestone. A little distance away, Horatio waited patiently. After a few minutes Hamlet lifted his head.

'Is that someone singing over there? In a graveyard?'

'It's the gravedigger, over on the other side,' said Horatio. 'I suppose it's just an ordinary day's work for him.'

'It must be a strange job, digging people's graves. Let's go and talk to him.'

Horatio had driven up to London to meet Hamlet, and on the way home they had stopped at St Jude's so that Hamlet could visit his father's grave. Hamlet looked pale and tired. The two of them walked through the long grass round to the other side of the church. By the wall was a deep hole, with a big pile of earth at one end. A bottle of beer and a packet of sandwiches lay on top of an old coat. The gravedigger was bent over, working at the bottom of the hole.

'Who's the grave for, then?' Hamlet asked him.

'Me, sir,' came the reply. 'I'm lying in it, aren't I?'

'Well, that's true,' smiled Hamlet, 'but you're also lying if you say it's yours. Graves are for the dead, not for the living.'

The old man stood up and rested his elbow on the edge of the hole. He drank some beer from his bottle and looked at Hamlet with interest.

Hamlet looked down into the muddy hole. 'Do you enjoy your work?' he asked.

'Why not?' said the old man cheerfully. 'I've been grave-digger here, man and boy, for thirty years. It's good, regular work. There's always plenty of dead bodies around.'

The gravedigger stood up and rested his elbow on the edge of the hole. He drank some beer from his bottle and looked at Hamlet with interest.

'Doesn't it worry you, working among the dead?'

'The dead don't frighten me, sir. Why should they? Rich man, poor man, girl, boy . . . they're all the same in a wooden box. And after a few years they'll just be earth again. Bones take much longer, of course. There's a lot of very old bones in this graveyard.' He finished his beer and bent down to the bottom of the hole again.

Hamlet picked up a handful of earth, and slowly let it fall through his fingers. He looked up at Horatio. 'It would be interesting to follow a body all the way through life, and death, and back to earth again. Who, for example, am I holding in my hand now, I wonder? Is it somebody I knew? Somebody I used to share jokes with?'

'I don't think those are either interesting or sensible questions,' said Horatio firmly. 'Come on. Let's go and find a nice cheerful pub with a lot of noisy, silly people enjoying themselves.'

But as they walked down the long graveyard, they suddenly saw several cars arriving at the gate. People in black got out and stood around, waiting.

'Oh dear,' said Hamlet. 'We'll have to wait until they've come in. Let's hide behind the church.'

After a time they looked round the corner carefully and saw the people walking slowly down the path towards the fresh, open grave. There was now some bright green, plastic grass tidily covering the pile of earth. The gravedigger had disappeared.

Hamlet stared. 'There's Laertes! And my mother, and Claudius! Who are they burying? Polonius?' he whispered fiercely.

'I don't know,' whispered Horatio, who knew very well that Polonius had been buried two days ago. A horrible fear was growing in Horatio's mind. He pulled Hamlet's arm. 'Let's go now, quickly, while —'

But he was too late. Across the graveyard the words were carried by the wind . . . 'this poor, sad young girl . . .'

'Oh my God! Ophelia!' Hamlet began to run across the grass towards the grave. Horatio followed quickly. As they came near, he saw Laertes look up and fix his eyes on Hamlet.

'You murdering devil!' Laertes screamed at him. 'She killed herself. And you're to blame. I hope you burn in hell!'

He threw himself at Hamlet and locked his hands around his throat. Gertrude screamed. Hamlet hit Laertes hard and the two of them fought like madmen. Then other hands pulled them away from each other and held them tightly. There were shocked stares and whispers.

Hamlet looked down into the muddy hole that was Ophelia's grave. Behind him, Gertrude came up and gently placed some white roses near the head of the grave.

'Poor, sweet girl,' she said softly. She put her hand on her son's arm. Laertes began to sob, a hard, dry sound.

Across the grave Hamlet stared at him. 'Well, Laertes?' His voice was dangerously calm. 'Do you think you're the only person who can cry for your sister's death?'

'Take it easy, Hamlet,' said Horatio quietly.

'Easy? I'll fight him if he wants to fight.' Hamlet's voice became louder. 'I loved Ophelia. I loved her more than forty thousand brothers could ever love her! Show me,' he shouted across at Laertes, 'show me how much you loved your sister!'

'Oh, he's mad,' cried Gertrude. 'Don't listen to him, Laertes! My poor son doesn't know what he's saying.'

'Let him think what he wants,' Hamlet said tiredly. 'It doesn't matter. Nothing matters. It's too late now.' He turned and walked blindly away.

Horatio took Hamlet back to his own small flat near the university. Hamlet said very little, but that evening he drank

'I loved her more than forty thousand brothers could ever love her!
Show me,' Hamlet shouted across at Laertes, 'show me how much
you loved your sister!'

most of a bottle of whisky. It seemed to have no effect on him at all. Ophelia's name was not spoken aloud.

◆

The next day Hamlet slept very late, until early in the afternoon. Horatio did not wake him. He was worried about his friend. Where exactly *did* the edge of madness lie? Horatio knew that his clever and intelligent friend was not mad, and had never been mad. But if you stretch a piece of string too hard, for too long, sooner or later it will break.

After a late lunch of bread and cheese, and a lot of strong black coffee, Hamlet seemed quite calm and cheerful. He looked round the untidy little flat, crowded with books and papers and comfortable old chairs.

'What a sensible man you are!' he said, smiling. 'A quiet life of studying, teaching, and writing books . . . and the university even pays you to study the things that most interest you.'

They sat down to read the Sunday newspapers together in friendly silence. After a time, Hamlet looked up from the business pages of *The Sunday Times*. 'I see Fortinbras now owns most of my father's computer company – controls it, in fact. Claudius made a bad mistake there. I've never met Fortinbras, but I hear he's a very clever businessman and a good man to work for. Unlike Claudius, who's made a lot of stupid mistakes. He doesn't understand the business world – all he wanted was the power, not the responsibility. And he spends too much money, on the wrong things.'

He laughed, and looked across at Horatio. 'Have you any idea how much it costs to arrange an "accidental" death? Ros and Gilly have been very expensive servants for him!'

'What's happened to them?'

'I told you on the way back from London yesterday. Don't you remember?' said Hamlet impatiently. 'They were going to deliver me to a bunch of very nasty gangsters in Toronto. You want a death? You pay for it, they'll fix it. Quick, easy, no questions asked. Road accidents a speciality.' He stood up and began to walk around the room. 'It wasn't very difficult. Ros and Gilly are quite stupid really. When we arrived, I got them both blind drunk, stole Claudius's letter from Gilly's jacket, and wrote a new one with their names in it, instead of mine. So they have the "accident", not me. There was a false bottom on Ros's suitcase and it was packed full of used banknotes – the first payment only, the letter said.'

Horatio watched as his friend walked moodily round the room, remembering. 'I left the letter and the suitcase with the money in it at the hotel front desk. It's the kind of hotel that doesn't ask questions. Then I went out and phoned the number in Gilly's notebook, from a bar. Twenty minutes later a big white car drives into the hotel carpark at the back. Four men go into the hotel, come out twenty minutes later carrying two bodies, and drive away. I took the train to Montreal, and got a flight home.'

'So Rosencrantz and Guildenstern are dead,' said Horatio quietly.

'They chose to play with fire – and they got burnt. Rules of the game, Horatio, rules of game. If you don't like the rules, don't play the game.' Hamlet's blue eyes were as hard as stones.

There was silence for a few minutes. Then Horatio cleared his throat. 'So what will this delightful uncle of yours try next, I wonder?'

'Surely, I've got a **moral** right to kill this man, haven't I, Horatio? After everything he's done . . .?'

'How soon will he get the news from Canada?'

'I don't know.' Hamlet continued his restless walk around the room. 'I'm sorry about Laertes, though. After all,' he gave a hard little laugh, 'why shouldn't he want revenge for his father's death? Revenge is quite fashionable at the moment, isn't it? I'll have to try and talk to him, and explain.'

At that moment the front door bell rang. Horatio went to the window and looked down into the street.

'It's Osric, your uncle's secretary.'

Hamlet joined him at the window. 'Oh God! He's a nasty little man – wears really horrible clothes.'

Horatio went down to the front door and returned, followed by a thin man wearing a shiny dark blue suit and a shirt that was painful to look at. His face was narrow, and his eyes were too close together.

'I suppose you've got a message for me,' said Hamlet pleasantly.

'Yes, Hamlet. Your uncle Claudius wants to arrange a reconciliation between you and Laertes. He wants both of you to forgive and forget the past. He's talked to Laertes, who has agreed. So he has invited you both up to the house to shake hands and have a drink together.'

Osric finished speaking, and Hamlet looked at the brilliant pink and orange colours of his shirt.

'That's a very beautiful shirt you're wearing,' he said.

'Thank you, Hamlet.' Osric looked pleased. 'It's Italian wool, you know. Made in Rome. Terribly expensive, though.'

'Ah yes,' Hamlet said seriously, 'but the Romans know how to make a good shirt.'

Horatio bit his lip, trying not to smile.

'So can I tell Claudius that you'll come?' Osric went on.

'When will this . . . reconciliation take place?' asked Hamlet.

'Now.'

'Now?' There was a pause, then Hamlet felt his unshaven chin with his hand. 'I think I should have a shave first, don't you? And perhaps put a suit on?' He watched Osric's face.

Osric looked at Hamlet's old jeans, and smiled politely. 'Shall we say six o'clock this evening, then? I'll tell Claudius.' He went out and a little later they heard the front door downstairs close.

'I don't like it,' said Horatio at once.

'No.' Hamlet stood up and stretched like a cat. 'No,' he repeated. 'It smells. It smells like a dead rat, in fact.'

'Don't go!' Horatio said urgently. 'Perhaps Laertes wants a fight. He can be a very nasty fighter – I've seen him.'

'I think I can win any fight with Laertes.'

Horatio looked at his friend's tall, powerful body. 'Yes, but . . . Well, I'll come with you and watch your back for you. But I still think you'd be wiser not to go.'

Hamlet smiled lazily. 'Do you see a great hand reaching down for me out of the sky? Or a mysterious rider on a pale horse, waiting unseen in the shadows?' His voice was calm, unworried. 'Today, tomorrow, twenty years' time . . . Does it really matter when the end comes? Why not meet death with a smile, and the hand of welcome?'

◆

They drove to the house in silence and walked up the steps to the door. Osric met them in the hall and led them to the library at the back of the house. Hamlet walked in, but Osric then turned and put his arm across the door, in front of Horatio. 'Claudius has asked me to say, sir,' he whispered quickly, with a polite smile, 'family only, you know.' The door shut in Horatio's face and he heard the key turn in the lock.

Inside the library, Hamlet paused for a second, then walked down the room. He nodded at Laertes, who nodded back, unsmiling. In the middle of the room, Claudius stood by a table, busily opening a bottle of champagne.

Osric looked at Hamlet's old jeans, and smiled politely. 'Shall we say six o'clock this evening, then? I'll tell Claudius.'

'It's good to see you, my boy,' he said. He poured some champagne into a tall, attractive glass. It was a deep, golden-yellow colour and a most unusual shape. 'This glass is for you, Hamlet. It's Venetian – four hundred years old. Very rare now. I want you to keep it afterwards, as a reminder.' He poured the rest of the champagne into ordinary glasses.

Then he moved towards the two young men. 'But before we drink to the future,' he said, 'perhaps a few words . . .' He looked at Hamlet.

'Yes, of course.' Hamlet smiled, and turned to Laertes. 'God knows,' he said simply, 'I did not want your father's death. It was a terrible, senseless accident. My only excuse is madness – I am my own worst enemy. I can only ask you to forgive me and —'

Suddenly, the door of the library opened and Gertrude came quickly in, followed by Horatio. Gertrude's eyes were bright and her cheeks were a little pink.

Claudius turned and looked angrily at his secretary, who looked back at him helplessly. 'I *did* lock it,' he whispered urgently. 'She must have another key.'

Gertrude had kissed Hamlet, and now turned to look at Claudius.

'Horatio's just told me about this reconciliation. Why wasn't I invited . . . to be with my son, and my husband? There must be no more fighting and arguments. I want to be the first to drink to this reconciliation.' She turned and smiled warmly at Hamlet and Laertes. Then she moved to the table where the drinks stood and picked up the tall Venetian glass – the one that was four hundred years old. Osric closed his eyes in horror.

Claudius stepped forward quickly. 'Gertrude, my dear,' he said calmly, 'not that one —'

But she had already lifted the glass and drunk deeply.

Across the room Claudius's eyes met Laertes' in a hard stare. Laertes took a slow step sideways.

'You're a little too quick for us, mother,' Hamlet said, with a half-smile. 'I haven't yet finished apologising to Laertes.'

He looked round at Horatio with a welcoming smile, and at that moment Laertes hit him. But Hamlet saw the movement out of the corner of his eye and turned like lightning. One hand seized Laertes' wrist and the other crashed into his stomach. There was a scream from Gertrude and Horatio ran to his friend's side. Hamlet let Laertes go and stepped back.

'Don't try a trick like that again,' Hamlet said angrily. He looked round and saw Osric's face, white with fear, and his uncle's heavy, watchful eyes. The silence was unnaturally loud.

Then Gertrude moved suddenly towards a chair and held onto it with both hands. Her face had turned very white. 'Hamlet! I don't feel well . . . It's the champagne,' she whispered shakily. 'I think it's drugged!' Her eyes closed and her body fell heavily to the floor.

Hamlet began to run towards her but he never got there. He did not see the kick coming, and Laertes' foot hit him in the back so violently that he was knocked to the floor. For a second he lay there, unable to breathe, a red fog of pain in front of his eyes. Then Laertes was on top of him and his hands were reaching for Hamlet's throat.

The fog of pain cleared from Hamlet's mind, and he knew that he was fighting for his life. Within seconds he had thrown Laertes off and was on his feet again, a mad light in his brilliant blue eyes. But Laertes, now in fear for his own life, pulled out a knife from inside his jacket and attacked fiercely. Hamlet jumped at him but Laertes was too quick, and Hamlet felt a sharp stinging pain deep in his side. He seized Laertes' hand and bent the wrist backwards until Laertes screamed in pain. Laertes' other hand hit wildly at Hamlet's face, going for his eyes, but Hamlet tore the knife away and drove it deep into Laertes' chest. Laertes crashed to the floor and lay still. Half-blinded and breathing painfully, Hamlet fell to his knees beside him. There seemed to be blood everywhere.

Then he heard Horatio calling urgently, 'Hamlet! I think your mother's having a heart attack!' Gertrude's face was now greyish-white and her lips were turning blue.

A dry whisper came from Laertes on the floor. 'Hamlet . . . forgive me . . . It was your uncle's plan . . . all wrong . . . too many deaths . . .'

Hamlet pulled the knife out of Laertes' body and, moving through a sea of pain, he jumped to his feet. He turned his eyes towards his uncle Claudius.

Revenge.

It was all over in a minute. So easily done, after all. Claudius had not moved. The knife did its work smoothly, and the heavy body fell forward onto the carpet without a sound. So easily done. Why hadn't he done it before, and saved all this trouble . . . all these deaths?

♦

At eight o'clock the next morning in Glasgow, Fortinbras was already in his office. The morning newspapers lay on the desk in front of him. BLOODBATH IN TYCOON'S HOUSE IN BRISTOL – THREE DEAD screamed the headlines. The reports were short because the police did not yet know the full story. They were hoping to interview the tycoon's secretary, a man called Osric, who had been seen at an airport in the early hours of the morning, trying to buy a ticket to Brazil.

The tycoon himself was dead, and also a young man. Both had been killed with the same knife – a kind of knife that can easily be bought in France. The tycoon's wife had died later

Hamlet, moving through a sea of pain, jumped to his feet. He turned his eyes towards his uncle Claudius.

in the night, from heart failure caused by a very strong sleeping drug. Another young man, the tycoon's nephew, was dangerously ill in hospital. The doctors did not think he would live for more than twenty-four hours.

Fortinbras drank his coffee thoughtfully. He was shocked and saddened by this news, but he was also a hard-headed businessman. Claudius and Gertrude were both dead, so all those companies must now belong to the son and nephew, Hamlet. Fortinbras had never met Hamlet, but he had heard good reports of him from a business friend who taught at Harvard. It would be very sad if Hamlet died . . . But if he did die, all those companies would need a new owner . . .

Fortinbras reached for the telephone.

◆

In a private room in Bristol Hospital, Horatio sat by Hamlet's bed and watched his friend dying. The doctors had tried to save him, but they had told Horatio there was no hope. There had been too much damage, too much bleeding inside the body.

Late on Monday night Hamlet became conscious again. He opened his eyes and saw Horatio bending over him. He tried to smile, but then the memories of those last terrible weeks came swimming back into his mind. So many deaths. Who would believe this horrible story? A death for a death. That was all he had wanted. A simple revenge, for his father's murder. He had no time now to explain that to the world. His eyesight was already failing, his heart was slowing, growing weaker. There were sharp pains in his side. He could feel Horatio's tears falling onto his face. His one true friend.

His voice was a ghostly whisper, painfully slow. 'Only you know . . . what . . . really happened . . . Horatio . . . Tell them . . . the world . . . the true story . . . if you can.'

His friend's hand closed tightly over his own. Hamlet said

no more. His breathing became quick and shallow, and soon death moved like a cloud of grey smoke through his mind.

◆

The trees round the graveyard of St Jude's church stood tall and black against the evening sky. The gravedigger had finished work for the day, and gone home to his supper. Above the church, the evening star shone with a clear cold light. The graveyard was quiet, still, peaceful. The dead do not dream, in the long silence of the grave.

ABOUT WILLIAM SHAKESPEARE

William Shakespeare (1564–1616) is England's greatest playwright and poet. He was born in Stratford-upon-Avon and went to London when he was a young man. There he became a successful actor and playwright, and later a part-owner of the famous Globe theatre. He wrote nearly forty plays, and most of them were seen by Queen Elizabeth I of England, and later, King James I. *Hamlet*, the first of his great tragedies, was probably written in about 1601.

Shakespeare's plays are still popular, and they continue to be acted, in the theatre and on film, four hundred years after they were written. The stories of the plays are both old and modern – they are about love, hate, jealousy, murder, revenge, greed, magic – and people in every century have found new enjoyment and new meaning in Shakespeare's works.

The Simply Shakespeare series retells the stories of the plays for today's world, keeping the names of Shakespeare's characters as a point of contact with the actual play. Other titles in the series are *Romeo and Juliet*, *Othello*, *King Lear* and *The Tempest*.

EXERCISES

Comprehension

Look at this chart. It shows the connections between Hamlet and the other people in the story. Fill in the rest of the names.

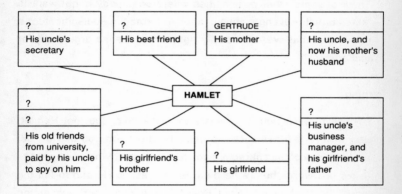

1 Out of the ten people in the chart above, only two people are still alive at the end of the story. Which two are they?
2 Write down the names of the eight people who died, in the order that the deaths happened.
3 How or why did these deaths happen? Were any of them accidents?
4 Write a short factual explanation for each death. The first one is done for you.

> POLONIUS *He was hiding behind a curtain, listening to a conversation between Hamlet and his mother. He was killed by Hamlet by mistake, because Hamlet thought that the hidden person was his uncle.*

Discussion

In Shakespeare's time plays about revenge were very popular, and people have always had strong opinions about the moral question of revenge – 'an eye for an eye, a tooth for a tooth, a death for a death'.

1 What is your opinion about Hamlet's problem? He knows that the law could never find Claudius guilty of murder. Should he let Claudius go unpunished for his crime? And what about Laertes? He, too, wants revenge for a father's (and a sister's) death. How is his behaviour different from Hamlet's?

2 Think of some other possibilities where somebody might want to take a private revenge, and kill another person in punishment for a crime. Can that ever be morally right? What are the arguments for and against?

Writing

1 Choose three or four characters from the story (but not Hamlet) and write a few sentences to describe them. Do you like or feel sorry for any of the characters you have chosen? Why or why not?

2 In his last words before he died, Hamlet asked Horatio to tell the world the 'true story'. Write Horatio's report for him, explaining why all the deaths happened. (Horatio, of course, is Hamlet's friend and will therefore be on Hamlet's side when he tells the story.)

3 Then write a second report by a newspaper journalist, who has no friendly feelings towards Hamlet. Imagine that the journalist does not believe in ghosts, and dislikes rich young men who drive fast cars and who think they can take the law into their own hands. He also thinks that Hamlet had an unhealthy relationship with his mother.

Review

The Tragedy of Hamlet, Prince of Denmark is possibly Shakespeare's most famous play. Every actor wants to take the part of Hamlet in the theatre, and more books have been written about this play than about any other play in the English language. For four hundred years, people have been recognizing themselves in Hamlet, and arguing about the complicated character of this unhappy and unde-cided Prince.

The character of Hamlet is central to the tragedy, both in the play and in this modern retelling. A different kind of man might take the advice of the ghost and kill his father's murderer at once. Then only one person would die, instead of eight. Look at these opinions about the character of Hamlet. Which ones do you agree with? Why or why not?

1 Hamlet is a weak and confused young man who cannot make a decision.

2 Hamlet is cruel to his mother and to Ophelia.

3 Hamlet cannot plan a cold-blooded murder; he can only kill without preparation, in the heat of the moment.

4 Hamlet cannot control his own feelings; he is very close to real madness.

5 Hamlet's real problem is his relationship with his mother.

6 Hamlet is an intelligent and thoughtful young man, who is caught in an impossible moral problem, to which there is no easy answer.

7 Hamlet does not really believe that revenge is morally right.

8 Hamlet does not understand women.

9 Hamlet's tragedy is that he can neither make himself kill Claudius nor forget his feelings as a loving son who wants to punish his father's murderer.

10 Hamlet is violent and moody, dangerous and irresponsible. He is a killer who feels no guilt.